Contents

Introduction 1
Blackbuck 6
Caracal 10
Golden Jackal 14
Black-Naped Hare 18
Black Marlin 22
Sailfish 26
Peregrine Falcon 30
Golden Eagle 34
Horsefly 38
The Fastest Snakes........................ 42
Spot Them Here! 46
Fact Finder and Credits 47

Need for Speed

Whether it is cheetahs chasing their prey across the savannah or peregrine falcons plummeting from the sky, speed is one of the animal kingdom's most incredible abilities. But have you ever wondered what makes these animals so fast and why they need to be speedy at all? Well, speed helps them survive in the wild. It comes in handy for hunting prey, escaping predators and migrating to new territories.

The caracal is a speedy cat found in dry parts of India

Fast Animals Have Aerodynamic Shapes

Aerodynamic is a word you are going to encounter often in this book. It is all about the way air moves around objects. Some shapes (think the kingfisher's beak) cut through the air faster with less friction or drag, and we say that's an aerodynamic shape.

What Makes Them So Fast?

The secret to superspeed in animals lies in their specialized body adaptations and powerful muscles. Some species boast long, muscular legs, while others have impressive aerodynamic body shapes built to reduce friction and maximize speed (think of the sleek shape of a fighter jet or your favourite sports car) that allow them to zoom past you in a blink of an eye!

Asiatic lions at Bannerghatta National Park, Karnataka

Why Do Animals Need Speed?

In nature, speed is a critical survival tool. Being faster than their prey is crucial for many predators. The Asiatic lion, found in India's Gir forest, is one such animal. They can run at upto **55 km/h** for short distances while chasing down prey like deer and wild boar. They are not the fastest cats, but lions hunt in packs and rely on both teamwork and bursts of speed to trap their prey.

Escaping Predators

Prey animals, on the other hand, rely on speed to escape danger. The blackbuck, an antelope native to India, is one of the fastest land animals, capable of running at speeds of up to **80 km/h**. When predators like wolves or tigers approach, it uses its quick reflexes and speed to outrun them and escape to safety.

A graceful blackbuck leaps across grassland

Blackbuck

Find Me Here!
In the grasslands and scrub forests of Gujarat, Rajasthan and Haryana.

CRITTER STATS
Scientific name: *Antilope cervicapra*
Size: 100–130 cm – like a motorcycle
Weight: 35–45 kg
Lifespan: 10–15 years
Habitat: plains, short grasslands and open scrub
Conservation status: least concern

Found in the plains of the subcontinent, blackbucks with their stunning black-and-white fur and amazing speed, sure are an impressive sight! The striking colour of their fur actually helps them stay hidden in their natural habitat.

They are easier to spot in motion as they bound across a grassland. Blackbucks run fast to stay safe from predators and cover large distances in search of food.

Until it was hunted to extinction in 1952, the Asiatic cheetah – the cheetah species native to India – was the chief predator of the blackbuck.

To stay safe and outrun cheetahs, blackbucks had to learn to run incredibly fast. Today, those skills are put to good use as they evade predators such as wolves and leopards.

The sleek blackbuck can reach speeds of up to **80 km/h!** And when pursued by an equally swift animal, they change direction superfast, making it even harder for predators to catch them.

DID YOU KNOW?

Blackbuck males put on a display in order to attract females. Males competing to win a female will lock horns and fight it out.

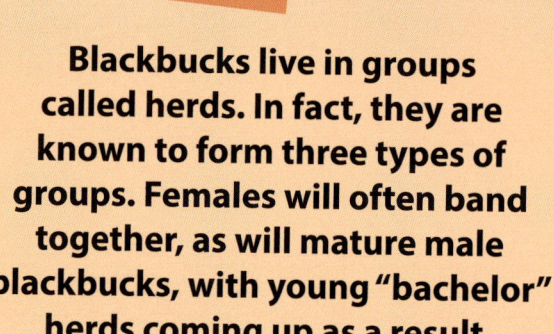

Blackbucks live in groups called herds. In fact, they are known to form three types of groups. Females will often band together, as will mature male blackbucks, with young "bachelor" herds coming up as a result.

Male blackbucks have cool spiral-shaped horns. These are never shed, and instead, keep growing through the entire life of the animal.

Caracal

Find Me Here!
Dry areas of Rajasthan, Gujarat and Madhya Pradesh.

CRITTER STATS
Scientific name: *Caracal caracal*
Size: 61–106 cm – like a medium-sized dog
Weight: 8–20 kg
Lifespan: 10–12 years
Habitat: arid areas, scrub and rocky outcrops
Conservation status: least concern

The forests and deserts of India are home to a mysterious feline resident, the caracal. It has a distinct reddish-brown coat and beautiful pointy black-tipped ears. But even more amazing than its looks are its unique superpowers of jumping and running!

*Image not from India

Unlike blackbucks, caracals aren't known for long-distance running. They are, however, known for their impressive leaping abilities.

Their exceptionally strong and long hind legs propel them up to 3 m (9.8 feet) high to catch birds or prey in mid-air!

And when it comes to sprinting, caracals can reach lightning-fast speeds of up to **80 km/h** for short distances.

Their quick moves help the caracal catch prey in a flash and make them one of the most successful hunters in the wild!

 DID YOU KNOW?

Caracals are so good at jumping vertically that they can swipe at birds mid-flight! Once a bird is swatted to the ground, caracals will twist their bodies mid-air to land on their feet.

Their large tufted ears aren't just for hearing better. They help caracals accurately locate prey, stay alert and focused while hunting and even help them stay cool in the heat.

These cats are extremely clever hunters. Their coats camouflage them effectively and their big, cushioned paws make them almost silent hunters.

Golden Jackal

Find Me Here!
Found all over India except in the Himalayas.

CRITTER STATS
Scientific name: *Canis aureus*
Size: 69–84 cm – like a German shepherd
Weight: 7–10 kg
Lifespan: 8–10 years
Habitat: forests, grasslands and even near cities
Conservation status: least concern

The golden jackal, with its golden-brown fur and sharp eyes, is often mistaken for a small wolf. It is a member of the dog family, and like other canines, it's known for being a great scavenger (an animal that feeds on dead animals) and hunter.

It is fast, resourceful and can outsmart many animals in the wild. Exceptionally quick on its feet, the golden jackal can run at speeds of **60 km/h** for short distances.

What makes them even more amazing is that they can run long distances at a steady pace – perfect for long hunts.

Golden jackals are great at working in pairs or even solo to catch prey or outwit other predators. On a hunt, jackals first locate prey using their incredible hearing powers before tracking it down.

Then begins the chase until the prey is all tired out. But our jackal has not run out of steam! It makes a final sprint at the prey and makes the kill.

DID YOU KNOW?

It helps to not be a picky eater! When they can't find prey to hunt down, jackals have no problems in picking at the remains of dead animals and even look for food around human areas.

This carnivore will even turn vegetarian on occasion, munching on grass, leaves and fruits too.

Black-Naped Hare

Find Me Here!

Found across India, from the foothills of the Himalayas all the way to southern India.

CRITTER STATS
Scientific name: *Lepus nigricollis*
Size: 30–50 cm – like a domestic cat
Weight: 1.8–3.6 kg
Lifespan: 4–6 years
Habitat: open scrub, farms and grazed forests
Conservation status: least concern

You're likely to spot a black-naped hare hopping around in the grassy fields and dry lands of India. With its long ears, big eyes and soft fur, this little hare looks adorable. But don't be fooled, for this creature has some cunning tricks up its sleeve.

When danger strikes, it turns into a lightning-fast hopper, capable of just disappearing!

Named after the black mark on its neck, this hare is a true survivor, using its speed to avoid predators and stay safe.

These hares can reach speeds of **70 km/h** when they need to, which is pretty fast for such a small animal. They usually run in a zigzag pattern, making it harder for predators to keep track and catch them.

Their long, muscular hind legs help them make quick, high jumps and fast sprints – all needed to make a quick getaway when danger lurks. Black-naped hares can leap over tall grass or obstacles with ease, using their powerful legs to spring into the air.

DID YOU KNOW?

These are not just fast runners – black-naped hares can also swim! They've been spotted crossing rivers and streams when escaping danger or searching for food.

These hares have quicksilver reflexes and can make sudden turns quickly enough to fool a predator.

During the mating season when hares pair up, males compete for females. This can lead to fights during which hares do some "boxing" using their hind feet.

Black Marlin

Find Me Here!

In open ocean waters of the Bay of Bengal, off India's east coast.

CRITTER STATS

Scientific name: *Istiompax indica*
Size: 380–465 cm – like a small fishing boat
Weight: 200–750 kg
Lifespan: 12–15 years
Habitat: open ocean, near surface, tropical seas
Conservation status: data deficient

Known for its long, sharp bill and sleek body, the black marlin is one of the ocean's true speedsters and an expert hunter. An aggressive predator, the black marlin's diet usually consists of smaller tunas, mackerels, squids, cuttlefish and octopus.

The black marlin holds the title of being one of the fastest fish in the world. It can swim at a jaw-dropping speed of **80 km/h**. That's faster than a car on an Indian highway!

Its sleek, torpedo-shaped body and long, pointed bill is perfect for cutting through the water, helping it chase and catch prey with ease.

The black marlin uses its bill to slash at schools of fish, stunning or injuring them to make the prey easier to catch.

 # DID YOU KNOW?

These migratory fish are great ocean travellers! They can swim huge distances across the oceans sometimes crossing entire seas to find food or suitable breeding grounds.

This fish has been around for a long time – the oldest fossil dates back 22 million years.

Sailfish

Find Me Here!

Off the coast of India and in the Andaman Sea.

CRITTER STATS
Scientific name: *Istiophorus platypterus*
Size: 230–300 cm – like a surfboard
Weight: 60–100 kg
Lifespan: 4–5 years
Habitat: offshore waters, near the surface
Conservation status: least concern

The sailfish is one of the fastest creatures in the ocean. With a tall, beautiful fin on its its back, which rises like a massive sail on a boat (that's why this fin is also called a "sail"), the sailfish is one of the most easily recognizable creatures in the ocean.

They are a part of the billfish family, which also includes black marlins and swordfish. The sailfish stands out not just for its appearance, but also its speed.

It can swim at speeds of up to **110 km/h**. That's almost as fast as a cheetah! Sailfish use their long, slender bodies and powerful tails to push through the water with incredible force.

Their sail – that long, high fin – can be raised or lowered depending on whether they are hunting or swimming at top speed.

When they're moving at their fastest, they lower their sail to reduce drag, allowing them to slice through the water.

DID YOU KNOW?

The sailfish's sail may also help it communicate with other sailfish. Plus, when the sail is raised, it makes the fish appear much larger, scaring off predators or competitors.

Sailfish are super hungry carnivores and feast on smaller fish and squid. They often slash through schools of fish with their bill to stun them like the black marlin does!

3,861 – that's how many kilometres a single sailfish travelled in 332 days! Sailfish travel far to get to warmer waters for breeding.

Peregrine Falcon

Find Me Here!
Look for hunting falcons around tall buildings, especially near open areas. Pylons along roads are a favourite perch too!

CRITTER STATS

Scientific name: *Falco peregrinus*
Size: 36–58 cm – like a school backpack
Weight: 0.90–1.5 kg
Lifespan: 13–25 years
Habitat: cliffs, open skies, urban buildings, coasts
Conservation status: least concern

The peregrine falcon is not just any bird – it's the fastest bird in the world! With its sharp beak, pointed wings and incredible speed, this majestic bird is built to hunt high in the sky and dive toward its prey at terrifying speeds.

Its aerial dives are one of the most amazing sights in the bird world.

The peregrine falcon is the ultimate aerial hunter. When it's flying high, it moves at about **55 km/h**, but the real speed kicks in when it goes into a powerful hunting dive.

During a dive, the falcon can hurtle down at speeds of over **380 km/h**! That's nearly the one-third the speed of sound!

It dives from great heights, folding its wings and using gravity to plummet toward its prey at breakneck speeds.

Once it's close, the falcon opens its talons and snatches its meal with incredible precision. Their sharp eyes and aerodynamic body design help them to maintain control even at such velocities.

 DID YOU KNOW?

Peregrine falcons have a special body shape that helps them zoom through the air. Their pointed wings and sleek, streamlined body reduce air resistance, letting them cut through the sky faster than any other bird.

These falcons have incredible vision – eight times better than human sight. They can spot prey from over 3 km away!

India has both resident and migratory species of peregrines. Some of these birds make long migrations – one falcon made a 9,000 km journey from Canada to Argentina!

Golden Eagle

Find Me Here!

High-altitude cliffs and mountains in Jammu and Kashmir, Himachal Pradesh, Uttarakhand and parts of Arunachal Pradesh.

CRITTER STATS

Scientific name: *Aquila chrysaetos*
Size: 70–84 cm – like a medium-sized suitcase
Weight: 3.5–6.5 kg
Lifespan: 20–30 years
Habitat: rocky cliffs, alpine meadows, open mountains
Conservation status: least concern

High in the mountains of the Himalaya, the golden eagle soars through the sky with incredible grace and power. This large bird of prey is a master hunter, using its sharp eyes and strong wings to hunt for food from high above.

The bird gets its name from the golden feathers on its head and neck.

While they are not aerial acrobats like the peregrine falcon, golden eagles are still very fast and powerful fliers. They can reach speeds of **240 km/h** during their hunting dives.

During a typical non-hunting flight, they cruise at around **80 km/h**, which is still as fast as a car on an Indian expressway. What makes them unique is their ability to glide for long distances without flapping their wings.

Their wingspan can be up to 2.3 m, allowing them to soar high above mountains, looking for prey. Once they spot a target, they swoop down with incredible speed and accuracy to catch it.

DID YOU KNOW?

Golden eagles have extremely sharp eyesight. They can spot a rabbit or other prey from a distance of up to 3 km away.

These powerful eagles hunt large prey. They can take down animals as big as foxes, wild goats and even small deer by grabbing them with their powerful talons.

Golden eagles pair up for life. They build large nests in tall trees or on cliff ledges, where they raise their young together. The parents take turns hunting and caring for their chicks until these are old enough to fly.

Horsefly

Find Me Here!

Seen in many wet areas across India including in Kerala, Karnataka, West Bengal and Assam especially during humid rainy months.

CRITTER STATS

Scientific name: *Tabanus spp*
Size: 1–2.5 cm – like a small coin
Weight: <0.001 kg
Lifespan: 30–60 days
Habitat: moist areas, near water, animal shelters
Conservation status: not evaluated

Though they may be small, horseflies are speedy little creatures with a serious attitude! These flying insects are notorious for painful bites caused by their sharp mouths. They're also known for being much faster and more aggressive than other flies.

With large, powerful wings, horseflies can fly at impressive speeds, and their victims find it difficult to escape.

When it comes to flying, horseflies can reach speeds of **80 km/h**! That's pretty fast for an insect, and it allows them to chase down animals like horses, cattle and even humans to take a nice juicy bite.

Their large, dark eyes help them spot their targets from a distance, and their speed makes it hard for their prey to outrun them.

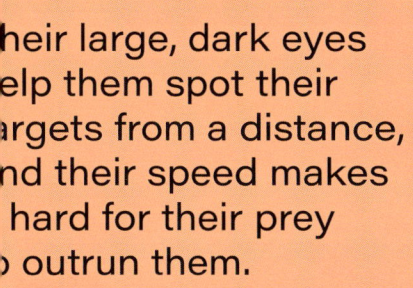

They're especially skilled at flying in straight lines and then darting suddenly to change directions. This makes them incredibly difficult to swat away or catch!

DID YOU KNOW?

Horseflies have sharp scissor-like mandibles (mouth parts) that cut into the skin to suck blood. These are designed to cut and scrape rather than pierce like a needle.

Only the females feed on blood! They need the proteins in the blood to produce eggs. The males feed on nectar and other plant-based foods.

Horseflies have super vision! Their large, compound eyes (made of many small eyes) give them nearly 360-degree vision – this comes in useful for spotting potential prey from far away.

The Fastest Snakes

Common Bronzeback Tree Snake
CRITTER STATS
Scientific name: *Dendrelaphis tristis*
Size: 100–170 cm – like a broomstick
Found in: most of peninsular India and Gujarat
Conservation status: least concern

Banded Racer
CRITTER STATS
Scientific name: *Argyrogena fasciolata*
Size: 75–130 cm – like a garden hose
Found in: most of peninsular plains, Maharashtra and parts of eastern India
Conservation status: least concern

Common Rat Snake
CRITTER STATS
Scientific name: *Ptyas mucosa*
Size: 200–350 cm – like a water pipe
Found in: across various regions throughout India
Conservation status: least concern

While they might not always seem like the fastest animals, some snakes are known for their incredible speed. Three of the fastest snakes are the common bronzeback tree snake, the banded racer and the common rat snake. Let's slither into their world and see how fast they really are!

Common Bronzeback Tree Snake

This tree-dwelling snake is built for speed, especially when it comes to climbing. It can move quickly through the trees and along branches, reaching great speeds. While that might sound slow compared to some land animals, it's incredibly fast for a tree-dwelling snake. The common bronzeback tree snake uses its speed to chase down small lizards and frogs, which make up the bulk of its diet.

Banded Racer

The banded racer is a fast-moving snake known for its speed on the ground. It can slither at speeds of up to **5 km/h**. What makes it especially impressive is its ability to maintain this speed over long distances. It uses its slender body and muscular frame to push itself forward with great speed. These snakes are excellent hunters. They can also react swiftly to threats, darting for cover when they sense danger.

Common Rat Snake

While not the quickest in short bursts, the common rat snake can slither strong and fast when it needs to. It can reach speeds of **16 km/h** on land, across open fields or through dense vegetation. This snake's speed is especially helpful when chasing down rodents such as rats and mice, which make up most of its diet (that's how it gets its name). It is known for its climbing skills and can also move quickly up trees and walls when hunting for food.

DID YOU KNOW?

The common bronzeback tree snake has a stunning bronze-brown body with a dark stripe running along each side. This helps it blend into the tree branches as it moves through the canopy.

The banded racer kills by constricting its prey or by applying body pressure.

Speed can be about more than distance covered. Research done on an American rat snake showed that they had a strike speed faster than F1 racing car!

Spot Them Here!

Follow the pug marks to find some of the best places to spot India's amazing wildlife! Animals such as the peregrine falcon, black-naped hare and the fastest snakes live across many regions of India.

Fact Finder

"Blackbuck Facts." *National Geographic Kids*, www.natgeokids.com/uk/discover/animals/general-animals/blackbuck-facts.

"Blackbuck (Antilope cervicapra)." *WWF India*, www.wwfindia.org/about_wwf/priority_species/threatened_species/blackbuck.

"Caracal." *Big Cat Rescue*, bigcatrescue.org/caracal-facts.

"Caracal in India." *The Hindu*, www.thehindu.com/sci-tech/energy-and-environment/caracal-india-threatened-species/article33684325.ece.

"Golden Jackal." *The Guardian*, www.theguardian.com/environment/2024/oct/02/golden-jackals-climate-breakdown-canis-aureus-western-europe.

"Golden Jackal: Wildlife Profile." *WWF India*, www.wwfindia.org/about_wwf/priority_species/threatened_species/golden_jackal.

"Indian Hare (Lepus nigricollis)." *Animal Diversity Web*, animaldiversity.org/accounts/Lepus_nigricollis.

"Indian Hare." *India Biodiversity Portal*, www.indiabiodiversity.org/species/show/265125.

"Black Marlin." *A-Z Animals*, a-z-animals.com/animals/black-marlin.

"Black Marlin." *Australian Museum*, australian.museum/learn/animals/fishes/black-marlin-istiompax-indica.

"Istiophorus platypterus." *Animal Diversity Web*, animaldiversity.org/accounts/Istiophorus_platypterus.

"Sailfish: Fastest Fish in the Ocean." *Ocean Conservancy*, oceanconservancy.org/blog/2020/07/27/sailfish-fastest-fish-ocean.

"Peregrine Falcon." *National Geographic Kids*, kids.nationalgeographic.com/animals/birds/facts/peregrine-falcon.

"Shaheen Falcon in India." *The Times of India*, timesofindia.indiatimes.com/home/environment/flora-fauna/shaheen-falcon/article/show/73219318.cms.

"Golden Eagle." *National Geographic Kids*, kids.nationalgeographic.com/animals/birds/facts/golden-eagle.

"Golden Eagle Sightings in India." *Deccan Herald*, www.deccanherald.com/national/karnataka/golden-eagle-sighted-in-niligiris-a-rare-visit-929380.html.

"Tabanidae." *BugGuide*, bugguide.net/node/view/314.

"India's Fastest Snakes." *Wild Charles Show*, www.facebook.com/WildCharlesShow/posts/indias-fastest-snakes/1170223768105486.

"Snakes of India." *The Hindu*, www.thehindu.com/sci-tech/energy-and-environment/fastest-snakes-india-cobra-racer/article65934770.ece.

Credits

Designer: Elisheba Samuel

Picture Credits

iStockphoto: Yash Darji, 2203824170; Kolbz; 172695099, 172695099; KenCanning, 1291077829, 1291077829; dtpearson, 146059584; NaluPhoto, 148443155; Liz Leyden, 155361624; sabirmallick, 155677986; grandrive, 181050446; Luis Beristain, 1313132540; Byron D, 525332657; grandriver, 181050446; NaluPhoto, 148443155; Lensalot, 1964835830; UJJAL SARKAR, 1405531553; Amit Shankar Pal, 1352911337; Yash Darji, 2203824170; Roop Dey, 1461228480; Sourabh Bharti, 1363247647; Sunil Mavidi, 1204084937; heckepics, 498999599; akspkoto, 475307372; Tariq Sulemani, 2196173059; Gerdzhikov, 2057426575; slowmotiongli, 1257180435; Rich Lindie, 1222025430; raksyBH, 1184563308; wrangel, 1132647580; Marcello Calendrini, 1130884783; StuPorts, 958697440, 472193905; eROMAze, 499262824; sabir mallick, 155677986; Kelly Dalling, 1329438563, 1199555262, 1169039758, 1085773052, 961604400, VSpillier, 522200359.

Pexels: Caracal image by Catherine Harding Wiltshire; 13140263 by Shyamli Kashyap; 929115 by Garuda; 2093459 by Erik Karits; 2028348030, by Jit Roy; 16440019 by Sandaru Muthuwadige; 442885112 by Aryan Gupta; 2278162 by Mike Singapore; 308962 by Vyok Khare; 270838 by Syed hasan mehdi; 1281014 by Nithin Shastri; 2751553 by Munna Mandalapu; 17173382 by Harsh; 3996823 by Estudio del Arts; 25130336 by Lasitha Kulatileke.

Unsplash: Sailfish by Michael Worden; Tabanus by Subhajit Das.

Wikimedia Commons: Banded Racer Argyrogena fasciolata by Ashahar alias Krishna Khan; banded racer 02, 03 and 04 by Shiv's fotografia; Bronze_backed_treesnake-Dendrelaphis_tristisby Anagha devi; Canis_aureuš_indicus_(Golden_Jackal_)_in_paddy_field and Golden_Jackal_(_Indian_Jackal)_canis_aureus_indicus by Shino jacob koottanad; caracal by Gopal Vijayaraghavan; Dendrelaphis_tristis_(4194698355) by Dinesh Valke; Horsefly_-_(28793243166) by Rison Thamboor; horsefly head by Shyamal; Indian_Hare_Rajkot by Dhaval Vargiya; Indian_Rat_Snake_-_Pytas_mucosus by Suniltalasila; Tabanus_07443 by Vengolis; rat_snakes by ChillionaireRohitgiri; Indian_rat_snake_from_kottayam_kerala by Deepugn.

Independent Contributors: Golden eagle in flight photos by Arpit Deomurari; golden eagle nest by Mohit Mehta; golden eagle by Uday Kiran; golden eagle photos by Irfan Jeelani; peregrine falcon photos by Amit Sharma.

Map: Syailendra Gupta Muliawan, India Vectors by Vecteezy.

First published by Juggernaut Books 2025

Text copyright © Juggernaut Books 2025

10 9 8 7 6 5 4 3 2 1

P-ISBN: 9789353458003
E-ISBN: 9789353455309

All rights reserved. No part of this publication may be reproduced, transmitted, or stored in a retrieval system in any form or by any means without the written permission of the publisher.

Printed at Nutech Print Services - India